no body in particular

no body in particular

Scrambler Books | Sacramento, CA

no body in particular
©2019 Giovanna Lomanto
Published by Scrambler Books
Sacramento, California
www.scramblerbooks.com

Cover art by Oriette D'Angelo
Cover design inspired by Elena Medel and the great Spanish publisher La Bella Varsovia.

ISBN: 978-1-7923-1036-2

You will
remember
we did these things
in our youth,

many and beautiful things.

from *Time of Youth* by Sappho

opening

there's so much i could tell you.
you are a stranger to me,
a blank slate,
and we will soon be filled with
scrawls and scratches.
and through our scarring, we will know
each other.

i.

when they ask me where i've gone

i am far away
and you are fast approaching.
we,
the two of us,
are set on a collision course
and we were destined to dream
of brighter days
and dimmer nights
and their intersections.
we were made
for the
in between.

i like the way the letter s sounds

somehow,
i am riding shotgun.
there's no driver
in my car,
and we are going nowhere.
the two of us sit,
stationary,
stagnant,
still.

between

i'm caught
somewhere in between
here and there,
dropped in the middle of anywhere
with empty hands cupped together,
pleading unapologetically
for answers.
what do i do now?

reconciliation

i think we are coming to terms—
at least, with each other.
i don't know exactly
why or how,
but i do know when,
and the answer to the latter
is a far more recent
than any other revelation,
but the two of us,
me and you,
are no longer
opposing forces
in this endless
tug-of-war.
now,
and only now,
we are on the same side.

what i wouldn't give

it is hard to admit
that falling in love
is an act of great sacrifice,
and however romantic you are,
no matter the semantics of your sentences,
i will love the words you say
because they have already consumed me,
and there is nothing more to give.

portraits

i can see the
lines
        you draw for yourself,
        and in a beautiful way,
        they are the perfect outline
        for who you are
        in my sketchbook
        filled with works of
art.

waiting

i cannot wait
until you forget me.

i cannot wait
until my name, or whatever
faded corner of my autograph
has yet to be smudged,
only ever comes with snaps and hums
as you balance on the border of remembering.
i cannot wait until my existence is barely,
if even,
an afterthought in your reveries
from a life you're sure was yours
once,
a long time
that feels like
and indeed was
ages ago,
in an eon survived by snippets of
surprise parties,
snorts of laughter,
scenes of revelation, enlightening
your self with the utterly breathtaking
concept of you,
a you before me,
a you with me,
a you after me
a you
i cannot wait

to never see.

the lies they told me

i think the word
past
is a deception in itself,
a misconstrued magnification
of intertwined interpretations,
an ever-present force
pushing itself into the
future.

end of the line

i don't know where i am
in the timeline of my being,
i have been on the edge of the end
for almost an eternity
and i exist
in all of my faults;
in fact,
i exist
because of all my faults.
and all of these
earthquake scars
leave me vulnerable beyond belief,
and i fear that one day
i'll split into sinkholes
and suck everything into a spiral
surrounding myself
and my sickness.
i've fallen somewhere
in between the cracks.
i'm still falling,
and i'm falling to the bottom.

going

i go places.
i go places without particulars
but go with prettied plans,
decorated in deceit and
carpeted with care.
i am in an impossibly inescapable
area of myself
that wants anything
but everything in front of me.
i am running;
i am running far and fast
but there is no finish
to the race
i am running,
and i am running
simply to go away
but now i am aware of my present apathy.
i am running
to go places,
and boy, am i living.

atlas falls

i am fully aware of
my capability,
my worth
to this world,
but that somehow
weighs me down
with such an incredible sky
that atlas himself would collapse
beneath
this hypothetically nonexistent
limit,
and so i
cannot breathe or move or function
underneath this impossibility,
and i am begging you to
quit your congratulating
and let me
collapse.

platonic

if i could bottle a moment,
i would put a stopper on these
shouts of delight,
hurried hugs,
and quiet conversations—
each a contradiction of its predecessor
but simultaneously a perfect fit.
i think it's wonder.
i think it's my ability to be
encapsulated
by incredible occurrences
and
i think
i've fallen in love
with loving.

ignore me again

i know you are no longer concerned
with the state
or fact
of my existence,
but i am often preoccupied with thoughts of yours.
i wonder if the sands you've stacked
have created the castle
you never believed you deserved,
but the royal treatment you so humbly bestowed upon
me
must be returned.
and until it is,
your highness,
you will be forever building
a separate sandcastle in my mind.

all i don't know

the bountiful unfamiliar
now keeps me at its beck and call.
i am a mere reflection of its orders,
a physical manifestation of every urging,
trotting slowly behind,
my pace labored and set by
a simultaneous apprehension and anticipation.

broken bits

i am
buried
in the business of beauty,
bound by a burden
unbearable.
i am
but a
broken bit of before.

something of substance

i am wary of
epiphanies
but of
soulmates
i am sure.

for even a moment

i think about the way you held me,
and i could almost believe
for a second
that i was yours,
that you were mine
and that our
interwoven bodies
were meant to fill
the empty space,
just for that moment.
i would be a fool
to entertain the idea of a forever,
so i'll instead indulge in our
temporality.

better days

i've been called an old soul
since i was young,
and i wonder if this theoretical
                             prematurity
has robbed me of a youth
i could have had,
        of an alternate reality
that might have saved me
from this over-romanticized
state of crippled living,
wondering when the years
between my body and mind
will finally collide in
the ultimate supernova of self.

painting

i told them
that my technicolor hurt,
that all the colors still scream my name,
and they demanded,
    insisted,
        required
            i listen.
i told them
that i could watch all the hues
converse in communion,
envying them all the while,
and they suggested,
    requested,
        informed me that
i need not worry.
in no time,
they would paint my vision
with a single shade of grey
and somehow
those words shriek with a color
        (or lack thereof)
that robs me
of the shade i painted myself.

early mornings

i remember
the outline of your figure
      curled close to mine
      for excited listening
and
the blur of your face
      snuggled deep in a pillow
      you grabbed to hug,
clearing my line of sight,
allowing for
the most beautiful focal point.

how i hurt

i hurt everywhere
    between the rattling of my ribcages,
    two jail cells to hold lungs that labor,
    who cannot bring themselves to function
    and
i hurt
    on the empty air weighing down my shoulders,
    barren where my ancestors bore burdens
    far heavier than I can imagine
    and
i hurt
    in the instances of movement
    when lifting my legs is a nearly insurmountable
    task that aches
    with every defiance of gravity
    and
i hurt most
    in the untouchable air
    between
    my head
    and
    my heart.

i wrote this for you

i see you
in book titles
and i wonder
how
you see me.
it seems that
whenever i see you,
i am in some way
sick,
but the beautiful thing about
us
is that
we see each other
(or at least i believe so,
and i hope that this sentiment
is seen).

where did you go

i am in
the thick of it
but you
are wearing me
thin.

resisting rusting

you live on the outskirts of yourself,
and i note your presence
rather than your absence.
not because "missing you"
is a nonexistent term in our vocabulary
but because outreach
is always an option.
conversation is a copper-coated
exchange of affection,
but ours is immune to rust
because you and i and we
care.
continue this,
please,
or i'll corrode.

hold my hand

if i could extend myself
to somehow find you,
to navigate without sight
in this extrasensory darkness,
i would search for your hand with my own
by pushing past the particles of empty air
between us.
and when i find you, you won't see me.
you have never seen me,
so instead you will interlace our fingers
until our palms pulse with pure energy
and we can see the surrounding sky.

spools

if you and i
run on a common thread
sewn into the fiber
of our clichéd being,
then i am honored
to walk the fine line
that strings our fabrics together.
and though
our material makeup may migrate
away from a central commonality,
we are nevertheless interwoven.
i fear we may one day
unravel.

tombstones

i'll start over until i stop.
i'll shovel handfuls
over my own grave
to prove i'm worth burying
and i'll dig until i'm done.

for you

i write letters
to people who will never know
i write for them.
hello;
this is yours.
these words belong to you.

**

i found where love stays

my first love lay
in the empty space between two pillows,
bright blue and deep purple
framing the corner of comfort
inside a square apartment
perfumed by my grandma's cherry lotion
and the fragrances from foods falling
perfectly into place on a table too full.

my second love lived
on the wooden planks of a backyard deck,
where tricycles circled a metallic table
not yet rusted over
and two tiny hands reached up to the sky,
waving goodbye to a nanny in an airplane
that took off months ago
but according to the kids
asking whether or not she could see
from all the way above the clouds,
the big old jet wouldn't set for years.

my next love settled itself in the border between two double beds,
a sliver of mattress just wide enough
for an extra girl to lie down,
listening to a familiar voice re-re-re-re-read
another one of her favorite stories
and ask if she could get a tracing to
press in the same folder as all of the

staple-bound books she wrote.

my next love developed
much more quickly than before,
nestled itself in the growing pile
of spirit shirts and color-coded pom-poms,
held on a special reserve for
photo ops and football games
or rallies and shows.

my next love dug its own hole
in a tiny black box theater,
never silent or still.
my next love found itself behind a keyboard
typing away at another
overly ambitious tale.
.
my next love rested
in the empty lift of fingers off of a piano
after a performance.
my next love crammed
the crowd of screaming concert goers,
always packed tightly in a too-small venue.

my next love lost itself
in an extroverted abyss of
introductions and awkward first conversations.
and now my next loves
could not be tallied with tick marks

or numerals—roman, arabic, or otherwise—
because my next loves never stopped growing.

i used to say
"i fall in love with places,
not people,"
but i am beginning to recognize,
realize
that these places are filled to the brim
with people,
with memories made or
to be made.
and i am ready to fall in love
again.

ii.

toy soldier

they say that i'm a soldier.
the battle scars on my
every extremity
are daily reminders
of every fight i've survived.
but all of this is past;
it is all past,
i tell myself,
but when the moon
shines her reflection
through my bedroom window,
the past becomes present,
and i am once again at war.
but the only enemy is my enmity,
my only opponent is
myself.
there's no great villain to defeat
except the one before you.
they say that if your eye
betrays you,
cut it out.
but what if the offending office
is all of me?
there is not an unbroken bit of me.
i am frankenstein's monster,
stitched together to satisfy a curiosity
and then abandoned.
i fall,
i faint,

i rise,
and i fall again.
they say that strength is not stability,
but my consistency is appalling.
i have always been a terracotta warrior,
meant to be buried deep below
and never touched.
they say that they come to life
to defend their emperor,
and here i am,
living,
breathing,
serving,
and i wonder if my enslavement
is eternal.
i try so hard.
i try so hard.
i try so hard
to understand
that i am more than the brittle
clay of my bones,
that the wars i fought were
all imaginary;
i've always been underground,
and there's a duty i must be
somewhere
fulfilling,
so what am i doing here?
they say that i am a light,

but what need is there for
a torch when every other
terracotta warrior
is paper mache—
flammable and flawed by design.
i've set the fire.
i've struck the matches
and i've done everything they've told me
at anyone's expense,
and i am over obeying these orders.
i am tired of fighting.
i have never held a weapon
with my virgin hands,
and yet i have the audacity
to call myself a combatant.
they say that you never
leave the battlefield,
but i'm not quite sure
when i stepped onto one.
all i know is that my first
step was on a landmine
and all of my terracotta temple
blew to ashes,
the very ashes that dr. victor frankenstein collected
and claimed to have created,
and he stitches me back together
again and again,
abandoning me at the battlefield
and returning to pick up the pieces

and start fresh.
i'm sick of starting over.
i look for the landmines now,
and each one sends an explosion through my skull,
rattling my brain
into a temporary hallucination
of satisfaction and sanity,
and then the doctor comes
to tell me once again
that i'm broken.
they say that what is broken can never be repaired,
and i must agree.
i am irreparable.
i am broken beyond belief.
i am nothing
but bindings,
and time is ticking
for this terracotta warrior.
they say she is strong.
they say she is loved.
they say so much.
they say so much they don't
even believe in,
so how am i to trust
that they believe in me?
they say that the terracotta warriors
are a treasure,
but the worth
of something is

packed in what compares.

a letter to my body

i remember how you used to feel.
i remember the concavity
beneath your chest.
i remember the smooth surface
over your abdomen.
i remember the fragility
of your every limb,
and i wonder
whether or not i should still miss you.
i don't think
we were built to last
because the fiber of our being
lay in a yearning for youth,
a tug from the temporary
that absolutely encompassed us
and attached itself
to our origins.
And i try not to meander
down the winding roads
of what could have been,
but i can't help myself
as i wander down
the paths dirtied by my own
muddy footprints.
i can't resist the familiar
face that is defined
by a bone structure so sharp
it could cut the tension in the air
that hangs between us—

between the "me" i am now
and the "you" you were before.
it pains me
to play with the past
but the plasticity of my brain
cannot process your passing.
i can't compensate
for all the care i couldn't give;
I am incapable of insensitivity,
they say,
but i cannot count
the compliments i deflected;
i cannot measure the moments of my madness.

now,
when i say madness,
i ask that you avoid
interpretations of my anger
and instead examine
the insanity
that erodes my intelligence
and exacerbates my irrationality.
after all,
i'm only an example,
and if i were a writing,
i would be an expository caution
that describes all the possible side effects
almost as an absentminded afterthought
because

i refuse to put you
on the forefront of my mind—or at least,
i'm trying to.
i am so desperate
to divide my past self
from you
because our memories
are irrevocably intertwined
and i am finally finding
that the frame
of our picture-perfect lives
lost its shine,
and no matter
how often i dust the edges,
there will always be
a layer of grime
greasing and graying
the black and white
that i've tried
so hard
to establish
between our good and bad,
and i wish
on every star in the night sky,
for either clarity or color
because these harsh outlines
are bigger than i can bear.
they envelope me
in an ever-painful embrace,

a too-tight hug
reminiscent of your unbreakable hold
on me.

although this nostalgia
never quite knows
when to go
away,
i think i need to
grow
beyond you,
in spite of you.
i've spent too much time tailoring myself
to fit the shape
of your ideals,
and it is only right
that i put the pin down,
that i work
to thread my own thoughts
into accepting the artwork that i am.
i think there will always be
a piece of me
that believes that you
were my one and only painter,
but i am so glad
you left the picture,
because now i can pick up the pen
you used to sketch.

in fact, now write with it.
now i write with you.

dear ed

dear ed,
i hated you.
i hated
how you would send soldiers
armed with needle pin pain
to the tip of my torso.
i hated
how you pushed me
into the bed of a shared
room that would have been empty
had it not been the two of us,
your thoughts racing
through my mind.
i hated
how i could never lift myself
after obeying your orders,
how you bore down
on my body until
i barely had one left,
and
i hated
how you pushed the word "no"
out of my mouth at
every one of opportunity's
attempts to reach
me—
me, i'm here; i'm just behind—

dear ed,
i loved you.
i loved
how you would sandpaper me
so thin
i collapsed
in a bloody heap
to be shipped off
to an emergency room.
i loved the questions, the attention,
how you managed to get
all eyes on me—
me, i'm here; i'm just behind—

dear ed,
i don't know what to think
of you
anymore
because it's easy
to hate someone you love
but it's almost impossible
to love someone you hate.
because of you—

dear ed,
do you know?
i was at the bathroom sink,
paper white towel pressed
against a blood red gash.

"i fainted," i told the boy,
scared, next to me.
"i look like a monster,"
i said, and i blame you for his silence.

dear ed,
what are we to do?
you will never die or disappear,
of that i am sure, but
the plot twist of this story
is that, i, too,
will stand firm in myself.
i know about you and me
in ways i never could have
imagined.
with you as my parasite,
dear ed,
we stretched to heights previously unseen
and i growing with an open air that greets
me and my body,
the body that you,
dear ed,
almost destroyed,
and though i harbor in my
heart a hurting,
i cannot say
in honesty
that i hate you
or

that i love you.

we are flying in turbulent skies,
dear ed,
and we will learn to soar
together.

gardening

i have grown.

i am growing
but i am reaching in all the
wrong directions,
veering left on a right turn only lane
and enveloping myself in the
welcoming embrace of the
crashing bushes
as they extend their open arms,
growing to chop and derail my own growth.
the flora around me
feel overly flamboyant
excessively exuberant

and i feel myself shrinking.

i shrunk.
i lost an inch this year,

and i lost so much more of
myself in this godforsaken garden
but when eve looks around eden,
all she sees is the beauty
around her, not within her.

eve and i are sinners alike,
tempted by the promise of better
only to find that better belongs

with a bitterness that bites.
it's a nibble.
it's a nibble of the serpent's apple,
and it's the most heavenly sensation
to have ever touched your tongue
and you see the obsession;
you understand why the taboo is
strictly forbidden because

an apple tree follows fibonacci's sequence.
it is a spiral,
and it closes in deep amongst
the extensive universe around,
but the apple is in your eye
and all you can see is this
forbidden fruit—

but oh, how dangerous.
if eve were to eat, if eve
were to fall for the temptation,
all hell would break loose
in the most literal sense of the cliché.

and i am eve.
i am in my hell.

i am in my hell,
still growing.
i am ashamed,

still growing.
i am broken,
still growing,
i am shrunken,
still growing.
i am nothing,
still growing,

and it is still a spiral,
a cycle that tightens in on itself
as it loops on and through,
deep and deeper
into the very ground i grew from
and in my hand is the core of
eve's apple,
and i drop it.
the apple follows the endless
spiral down,
and tears trickle down the
tears and hollows of my skin,
spiraling down,
spiraling down
until every spiral meets the other
and something

blooms.

quietly, deep beneath the
beauty of the garden,

a blossom,
my blossom
sits dug in its own
little cove,
so far away from the
flashy flowers above,
and it is mine.
it is isolated and it is mine,
and as i walk down the
spiral to meet it,
i am mine,
and when i find the petals and the greenery
of what was once a sinful apple
and i hold her,
i hold myself
in the palm of my hand.

i look up, and i am everything in this
nothing i have made.
i am nothing in the garden above,
but the garden above is not mine.
i have fallen,
but i have fallen of my own fault
and if i grow,
if i outstretch my arms
from the bottom of this pit,
i will be all sticks stitched
together,
and i have been that,
and i will never be that
again.

and eve is in her grave.
i am six feet under at
the point of the spiral, and
no spring awaits me at the bottom
to shoot me up and out again.

no, i must reach.
i must stretch.
i must break.
i will break.
and, oh, will i be beautiful.

unreal

there's a sort of safety
in anonymity,
and it wraps me,
      encapsulates me
in its embrace.
i open my own arms
to greet it wholeheartedly
as the organ of mention
pumps to
pervasively
that my body overflows,
overwhelmed.

but the beauty of such a sensation
lies partly in the fact that,
in someone else's fairytale,
i am fictitious.
i am fragments of projected adventures.
i am nobody,
and being this nobody
is a shield of its own,
protecting my
self
from any possible sabotage.
maybe this pessimism is pointless;
maybe my worries mean more
than preemptive measures,
but i'll always
make my moat

an imperceptibly imperfect
impossibility to cross.

there's no simple
drawbridge of doom,
opening the castle doors
to the doom of our destiny
to be vulnerable—
instead,
I have installed an infinitely insignificant
tight rope
so small
that it sparks a fear
in anyone who starts to see it.
and anyone who
comes across
must unburden themselves
of their own shortcomings
to enter the castle
clean
of protections
and littering their faults
on the floors before
my feet.
because i am the castle.

i am the bearer of belonging,
opening my arms the way
anonymity

opened her arms to me,
enveloping anything that gets
too close to its center,
rumored to be stuffed with centuries' treasures.
but in reality,
i,
the castle,
am ruin.

a word alone

nostalgia
(a word alone)
cannot capture
relentless tirades in the land of longing,
nor can it encompass the depths of a desperate
wish for a past romanticized
a life lived not far away
and not long ago.

if i were to blink
as the vehicle veers down this
precarious pathway,
i might miss the
rolling fields that separate
the trough from the valley,
but whenever i consciously close my eyes
i still see the same stretch,
as if the dull plateau
scratched itself a space on my pupil
so that my eyelid could never
push it out of position
so that it secured the permanence
of imperfection.

with a steady slope of zero,
i climb up this terrain,
and though my elevation never escalates,
the rugged roughness of it all
pulls me past the point

of failure
but never quite in the direction of success—
no,
rather,
it taunts me as a cruel reminder
of not what
could have been
but, instead, of what
should have been.
i catch myself here.
i catch myself in this tension,
 in this present tension
in the present tense.
as much as it pains me
to speak of the past in passing,
i cannot reconcile who i was
with who i now am
save for one statement:
i am a monster.

i am a monster
who only seeks to wreak havoc
on herself.

i am monster
who uses her strengths to exploit
herself.

i am a monster

who has a cunning urge to manipulate
herself
until her self
cannot identify a time
in which self-sabotage sat in the
backseat of the veering vehicle,
and she closes her eyes
to look away from the plains
between peaks and valleys;
she closes her eyes
and she crashes.
she is crashing—
present tense.

crashing
(a word alone)
can capture the essence of
this monster.

my therapist told me to write this

i would like to say goodbye.
i would like to
bid my farewell
to thin arms and thigh gaps,
to
collapsing collarbones and
small sizes
but I realize
that this is a point of view.
i am skewed.
i am swollen and swallowed whole
by the stretchmarks
spreading across my skin,
sprawling across expansive areas
that are bigger than before,
and i am entirely alone,
isolated on an ice cap
melting into the
big black sea
that i have cried myself
in mourning of
my attachment to a body
that never belonged
except to me.
and oh,
did i love it?
did i deeply
cherish checking to see if my
cheeks

were hollow enough?
did I carefully
compose the cacophony
my bones would make
when they rattled against each other?
did i?
do i?
will i?
if i do,
who am i?
i wrote a poem
about my monstrosity,
but i think that
that is
what makes me human
and whole.
i have pushed myself past
billions of breaking points,
but i now see the strength of my bending.
i see the beauty in believing
that i am the damned;
      i am the desolate;
      i am
dying,
here and now,
always and forever
in this endless emptiness
that grows inside me,
and i am expanding beyond belief.

i push my limits
until i am
nothing more than
the outlines i allow
to define me.
and then i shrink.
and then i disappear.

capital letters

i have always wanted to be something.
(something,
capital s).
i fell in love with the stars
when i was just a little girl
and i used to count the pinpricks of the sky
as if somehow,
(somehow,
capital s)
somehow,
i could reach a number
that would alter the science of my being
so that i, too,
could shine through the twilight
and disappear in the daytime.
i could come and go as i please,
flicker in and out
and i could see the world from end to end
and still
(still,
capital s)
go on.
i could turn myself to dust up there
and nobody would notice.
i'd just be an erased mark
on a cartographer's mark,
giving his mind the space
(space,
capital s)

to ponder new projects.
in fact, i would fuel
further discovery
because energy is neither created
nor destroyed
and every vibration in my bones
will shatter
(shatter,
capital s)
this awful atrocity
that god forgot to give a purpose—
but no matter.
she is small
(small,
capital s)
and she will soon be with the stars,
a speck in the sky,
a moment monumentalized
and she will be nothing
(nothing,
lowercase n).
she is nothing.

a fantasy

i will never forget the sunset,
the soft light colored
in hues of orange and purple.
the image of your sloped shoulders,
the sound of quiet assent
assails my senses
in an endlessly
inviting endeavor.
i remember how you called
how my words beautiful,
how an offhand compliment
somehow signified satisfaction,
and in such a visceral,
eternal memory,
i am reminded of our first meeting,
an extended conversation
with a charming man whose
pursed lips and guarded smile
enveloped every utterance
with a confidentiality
to be held sacred.
and i strayed.
if you were holy,
i was the prodigal,
leaving and returning in shambles
for the broken pieces of myself
to be in some way celebrated,
but the grand scheme was a
natural occurrence of events,

coincidences in coffee shops,
analyses of the invented.
but we were not tangible.
i could detail every smile
i sent your way,
every giggle
i choked out
(or alternatively tried to silence),
and it would still not serve
as justification for the
colors i've cloaked you in.
i cannot call this infatuation
love,
nor can i call it anything less,
and, oh, this has become an ode
to the order that we uphold
ever so easily.
you are a fool to think me foolish,
though i am the fool to think
i fell.
i have fallen deep below the ground
before i even laid eyes on yours,
sparkling, enchanting—
and i am in more pain
than i will ever let you see,
even though you will never ask.
i have a slough of questions
for you,
but all that you have for me

is an obligation for decorum.
i want to know your every
intricacy, and i want you to know
that i am entirely insignificant.
you will forget me.
but i will remember you.

live with the uncertainty

if I could pigeonhole uncertainty
to the sole title of enemy,
there is no doubt in my mind
that a half of me would,
that a good portion of my being and vision
would rob myself of spontaneity,
favoring security and solace
over the sensation of celebrating
every extraordinary expedition that occurs
entirely unplanned.
and if
truly
the best things in life
(a phrase so often abused and misused)
are those we don't see coming,
why am I always checking the
rear view mirror
and watching through the corner of my eye,
waiting for a vision in my peripheral
to materialize as an imminent danger?
why am i anticipating accident?
                      incident?
                      injury?
as i clutch the beloved steering wheel,
clenching until clammy palms
create a slick barrier
between myself and the controls—
that is, before i sacrificed them entirely
because i couldn't handle the heat

i would feel behind my ears
on that open road,
a sacrifice i believed would help
but has only hindered,
another testament to the mental revolution
whose war cry is that:
if i could call uncertainty my friend,
i would.

you were my captain

sometimes i wonder if you ever knew
just how deeply
you plunged,
headfirst.
i say headfirst
in your case
because you had full knowledge
of your affect on me
and yet
you were somehow incredibly oblivious.

do you know how i felt
that valentine's day?
i was sixteen.
i was sixteen when you decided
to upend the ship
i was so carefully building
with you as my imagined captain,
and you sunk us.
you left me,
stranded,
while you explored new oceans
with newer, better ships,
and i could feel the planks
beneath my feet
creak;
i could hear the sound
in the silence you left.

there are days that i look back
in my own reverie of shame
and wonder how i let
a pirate
commandeer the navigation
of this builder,
and I think that,
even if i exchanged there
wooden boards for bricks,
you still would have found a way
to carelessly pillage
me for all i had
and leave my ground
desolate
while you floated off to
your next adventure.

for a long time,
for the longest time,
i sorely hoped
that someone would
fire cannonballs into your side
and that the wide oceans
would swallow you whole.
but when you raised
your white flag,
if only for a moment,
i realized that you might miss that land
you left behind.

if you ever decide to turn back,
i'll be there,
building a new ship.

no goodbye

i know that
the nature of us is temporary and that,
despite our painstakingly detailed history,
our future together is finite,
and one day,
 maybe soon,
i will not know you
anymore,
and you might forget the crinkles,
the creases
in the pages of each other that we pored over,
knowing that the possibility of
            pouring rain
might wash the clean space
between the lines of ink
until everything we knew
became an unintelligible blue.

here.
here is a pencil,
a graphite graphic i beg you to use
in our
soon to be separate lives,
a ubiquitous utensil
that will bear an unknown meaning
as you scrawl new scenes
into a sketchbook
devoid of my existence,
and i can only hope that

in your frantic frenzy of recording
every freckle on the unfamiliar face
across from you,
far from me,
i can only wish
from wherever i am,
that you'll look at the trusty tool
set so deeply in your palm that you
sometimes
forget your hand is full,
that you'll feel the damp pages
of a shelved journal that you
sometimes
forget you own,
that you'll connect the two,
not just in your mind,
but on a map,
and that you'll find your way
back to a memory of me.

ear plugs

flashing lights and fog
frame your silhouette,
draped against the backdrop
of your own design,
a stage
(both figurative and literal)
created,
it seems,
just for the moment,
a serenade of sound.
oh, god
does it move my bones,
sending the vibrations through the
gaps between my ribs
until i cannot distinguish palpitations
from pounding sound—
not unpleasant,
no,
your melodies and the sweet cinnamon honey
of your voice
could never leave a bitter aftertaste
and I'll always reach for more
of the raw emotion
so tangible that it
poisons
the joyful overwhelm
i see painted on your face,
your sweat-stained features
struggling to be seen under spotlights.

but my arm extends
to meet yours,
or at least i think it does
because i cannot see through this haze,
and i hear a shrill cheer,
an abandoned voice repeating studied verses
choruses to songs i think i played on repeat,
but i cannot be sure
since this body,
these senses are not mine,
wish though i may,
and maybe
that is part of your allure.
maybe i love you
because you can love,
and i think i can see it.

footsteps

sometimes, when i close my eyes,
i dream of you.

i dream of your sprawling streets,
crisp-white bedsheets,
foggy skies,
floating eyes,
romances encompassed by couplets
and set so deeply into
the stone of stereotype.

you are a place.

you are uncharted territory
and i did not believe
in the manifestation of knowledge
until i met you.
i first met you
years ago,
but i am still meeting you
to this very moment,
and every additional ounce
in your measurement
is anything but
overkill,
and each breath of knowledge
is a simultaneous step into history.

i am you,

and we are an amalgamation
of all we have done
and will do,
of all we have seen,
and will see.
of all we have heard,
and will hear.

we are united by choice,
the two of us,
and i am eternally grateful
for paved pathways
and all those who walked on them
before me.

you and i are inseparable
and yet entirely unidentical,
and that is precisely the beauty
between us.

we belong together.

you are full of promises
and i am full of promise,
and we,
together,
are complete strangers
with an intimate knowledge of each other's
whereabouts and wanderings

as if we had held hands
through every leg of this expedition.

we belong
(not with but)
to each other,
this land and my soul,
because the moment
i lay my ear onto the streets,
i can hear your heartbeat.
it sounds like footsteps.

for you, rachel

both moments and years ago,
elegies honored the dead.
and on such solemn situations,
mourning is most magnanimous a gift
from the incomprehensible winds
that somehow shifted our sails
until we were set on a collision course.
and what beautiful oceanic expanses we filled
with our overflowing insecurities
as our rudders steered with
encouraging affirmations.

but somehow
by the power of pacific currents,
we stayed afloat
in the midst of misty conditions
filled with contradictions
and truths
and discoveries—
like the oyster you held
in the palm of your hand,
both open with and to the possibility of pure beauty.
you held and we beheld the gifts you presented.

we held and beheld
the gift of your presence,
and i only wish that those moments
could expand to eternity.

but ships are not safe from sinking.
and i worry that our dislodging will
summon a deadly vortex
that sucks you back into the depths
of your treasure map's trail,
not for the pain
or for fear of the splintering planks and my crew,
but for the sheer amount of selfishness
that wants you to stay the course
and veer off the path prescribed.
i wonder which would be best.
and i realize that your treasure map calls.
it is beautiful, and it
demands
the completion of its circuit,
so I step aside in this expanse of sea,
hoping—
knowing
that you'll find other ships,
torn before or even because of you.
while i am jealous,
i am honored
to have joined in their ranks.

you think too much for this highway

my mother tells me that i think too much.
she tells me that the highway of my thoughts
has an unrealistic speed limit
for the heavy load in gas guzzling
commercial trucks
whooshing the long way
across roads that could span centuries,
running circles without a word of what
eon the calendar proclaimed the present to be;
no directions existed besides
forward.
forward was the only sight in this
tunnel of vision
clouded by the cars' coughs into once-crisp air
until the beauty of a dewy morning,
the hour of an early fog
through the window threatening to crack
became morning smog,
a haze with no beauty,
         no purpose,
                  no redemption
for the haste of such
promising pieces of public infrastructure,
too crowded because the accountant
couldn't catch the cash from the drivers
who no longer stopped at toll booths,
but threw handfuls
out open windows.

impossibilities

i cannot love you—
and i say this
with the same finality
that crosses our stars,
that finishes our friendship
and leaves it as said.

but the words
that cannot leave my lips
somehow slip
between my teeth
despite my attempts to contain
these expressions of the ecstasy
i feel around
you.

no,
i cannot think of
our experiences,
of
your existence
because i cannot love you.
i will not
fall deeper in love with you.
this chasm
is bottomless
and i have somehow
hit its pit.

i see you
driving yourself up and out,
your hands gripping
the ten and four of your steering wheel
as you maniacally maneuver around every obstacle
placed to keep you at arm's length
and
as i
run away in my fear
from any possibility
of the finite future
that might find itself in fruition,
and i find that,
no matter how nonsensical,
i would rather spend eternity
at our opposite ends
than even entertain,
the idea
of us
in emptiness.
i cannot love you,
not because of its impossibility
but because
it is a probability
and i cannot love
our numbers.

possibilities

i will write you a poem.
one day,
in a near distant future,
i will dedicate a didactic
to the dissonance
in the gaping gap between us.
maybe it'll be late one night,
and i'll pull out a pen and paper
to read you a simple sonnet.
maybe you'll slip into a smile.
maybe you'll fasten your fascination
on every facet of my phonetics
and maybe,
just maybe,
i'll leave a lasting impression
on your life.
i hope that
(maybe)
you'll look back longingly
at the memories of our moments
and maybe,
just maybe,
we will let our facades fall
fast and faster
until they tumble down
in their own time.
until then,
i will daydream of the
distance that will

soon separate us
and make up the miles
of moments i will send to you,
because i am so scared
to lose something special
because of all this empty space.
i am dimly determined to drive
myself on the open road
away from everything in this town
except for people.
i will miss them.
i will miss you.
and maybe,
just maybe,
i won't have to.

***

you and yours

there are moments,
slivers of a person that stack
onto the wrapped gift that is their self,
    moments i don't want to forget.
you:
i saw you in the corner of my eye before I moved
and saw you tucked in the pocket of a social circle
before it spun on the axis of
forced coincidence,
which kindly placed us side-by side
        eye-to eye.
you:
i heard the musicality of a teenaged boy's reedy voice
before i noticed the ghost of a whistle
hurdle between your words
in the instances you weren't
stifling a laugh.
you:
i felt the shake of your shoulders
before i realized yours had bumped into mine
yet again,
and chuckled at our clumsiness,
nudging each other in joint enjoyment.
you
are full of moments
and i'm glad i could live in some.

iii.

go on

there is a rhythm in music,
infectious beats standardizing, regulating
every sound.
the tempo changes within
the metronome's restrictions,
a single pianist
falling behind
as the orchestra continues,
and the band keeps time
without her.

bruising

the morning itself is black and blue,
bruised by the very idea of noon
dispelling the gentle caress
of dawn's soft light,
but this victim is
(or might be;
there's never much certainty)
saved by a cloudy hero
and his outpouring
of torrential tears.

let's take a hike

there is something between a city's
sparkle and shine
from up above—
and it is the coast cutting beneath bridges
in an all too familiar abyss of brightness,
each headlight housing a driver,
each building hovering over who knows how many
street walkers
obeying the greed/yellow/red of intersections
or launching across the way regardless.
all of this is speculation,
an assumption from this removed virus.
all i see is that this is home to
a cold bench beneath a group of new friends,
a girl elbowing the boy next to her
and muttering something under her breath,
a forest of trees framing a virtually vertical hike
and a small breeze
whisking something away.

gray space

neutrality is no longer a choice
but rather
a habitual state
that occupies the ground
between extremes,
the resting place of a pendulum
that seems to swing somewhere on the border
of never
and always.

rear view mirrors

how strange
and absolutely arresting it is
to forget your heart
and to neglect history
in the favor of a folly.
how odd
and incredibly abnormal it is
to live a lifetime
and not look back.

acknowledgements

I would, first and foremost, like to thank my family. From parents who stayed by my side (literally and figuratively) to a sister who never let me get away with anything, from grandparents at home to aunts and uncles abroad, I have been blessed with an incredible support system. Second, I would like to thank my friends. Some of these poems are for and about you, and though I don't have the space to name each of you individually, I want to express my gratitude for your love. Third, I would like to thank my publisher/editor extraordinaire Jeremy for making this book possible. Fourth, I would like to thank all my teachers and mentors—from elementary school to college, you have greatly influenced my life. Fifth, I would like to thank everyone who has contributed to building my faith. in doing so, you have strengthened a part of me that allows grace into my life, and I am incredibly blessed to have supporters who encourage me to grow spiritually. This book would not exist without the care and consideration of everyone in the above, and it is with this statement that I list my final acknowledgement: you. If you are reading this, I want to thank you for doing so. Thank you for listening to my stories.

bio

Giovanna Lomanto is a poet hailing from the expanses of Californian suburbia. When she's not scrawling poetry into her journal, she's often having long conversations on the phone with her friends and family, walking around bookstores and art museums, sipping hot cups of Earl Grey tea, making playlists for her favorite songs, and cracking cheesy jokes. Giovanna is currently pursuing her BA in English at the University of California, Berkeley.